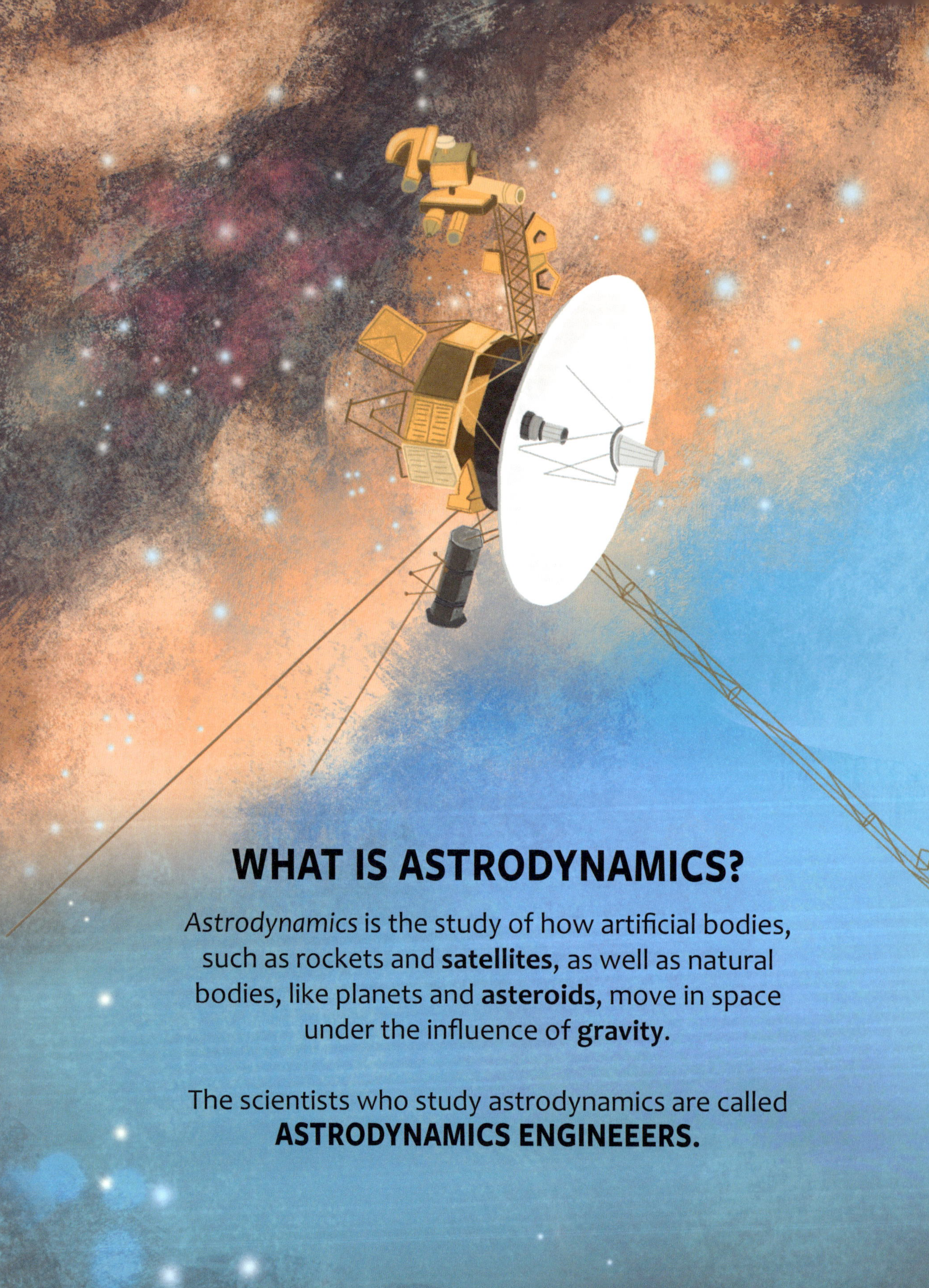

WHAT IS ASTRODYNAMICS?

Astrodynamics is the study of how artificial bodies, such as rockets and **satellites**, as well as natural bodies, like planets and **asteroids**, move in space under the influence of **gravity**.

The scientists who study astrodynamics are called **ASTRODYNAMICS ENGINEEERS.**

HOW DO SPACECRAFT GET TO OUTER SPACE?

DISCOVER THE SCIENCE BEHIND **ASTRODYNAMICS**
(AST-roh-dye-NAM-iks)

Written by Eliza Jeffery
Illustrated by Verónika Cháves Morales

Words that are tricky to understand are in **bold**. Find out what they mean in the glossary.

Words that are difficult to say are in *italics*. Find out how to say them at the back of the book.

Humans have always been curious about outer space and have wondered if, one day, we could travel there. The invention of spacecraft was an exciting way for scientists to learn new things about the mysterious places in the sky.

One of the first spacecraft ever launched was the unmanned Sputnik 1, an **artificial satellite.** It was a big deal when **human-made** vehicles

first reached outer space!

Reaching outer space is only possible because of scientists' understanding of gravity. A man called Isaac Newton discovered gravity by watching apples fall from a tree.

Astrodynamics engineers today use what they know about gravity to design spacecraft that can leave Earth's **atmosphere** and not only reach, but navigate through outer space safely! After the success of Sputnik 1, scientists began to think bigger…

Soon, scientists created a spacecraft that could
carry humans to outer space!

The Apollo 11 Lunar Module was the first **crewed** vehicle to land on the Moon. This was an incredible achievement for scientists all around the world.

So, we know it's possible for spacecraft to be in outer space, but how do they actually get there?

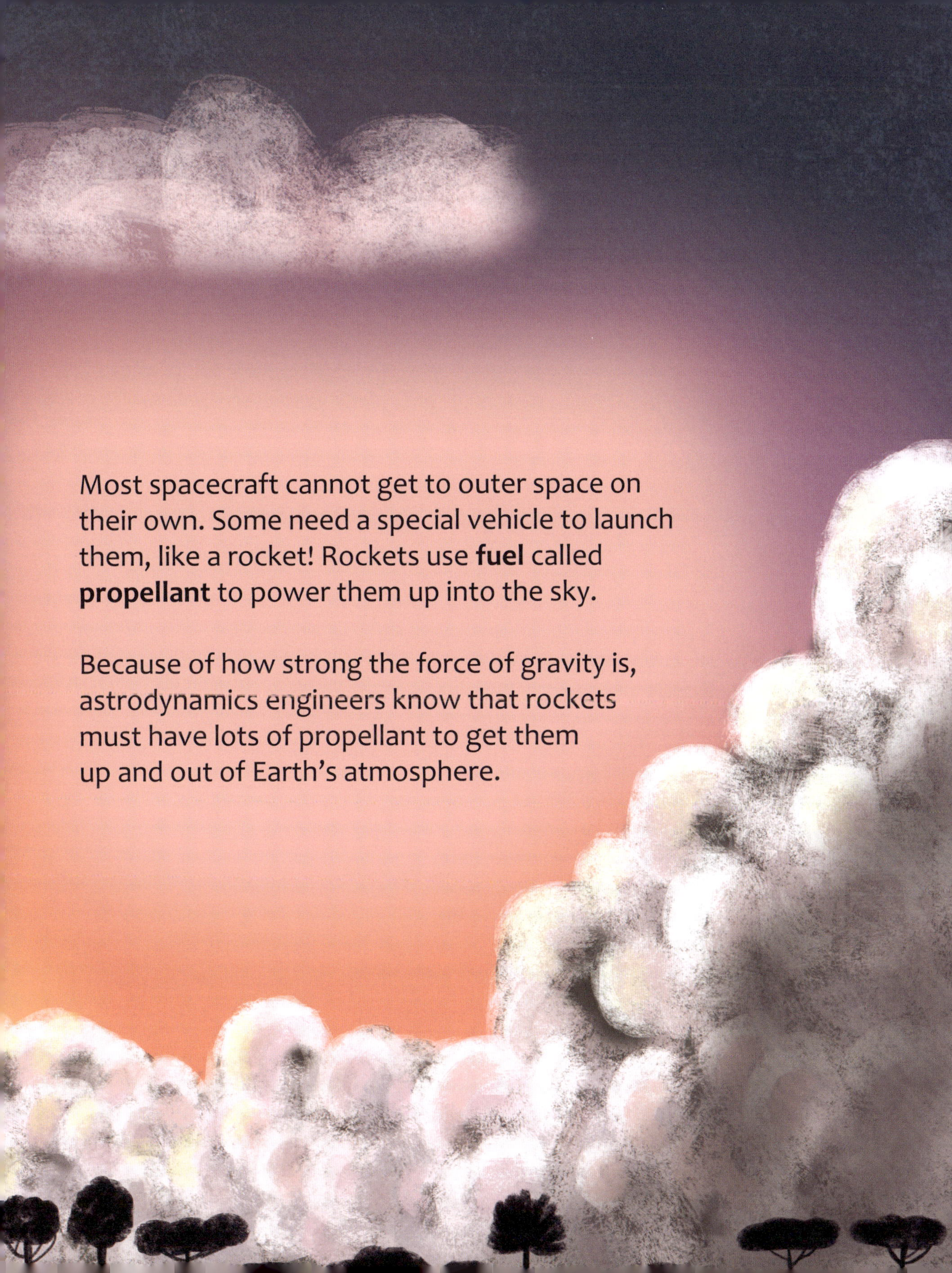

Most spacecraft cannot get to outer space on their own. Some need a special vehicle to launch them, like a rocket! Rockets use **fuel** called **propellant** to power them up into the sky.

Because of how strong the force of gravity is, astrodynamics engineers know that rockets must have lots of propellant to get them up and out of Earth's atmosphere.

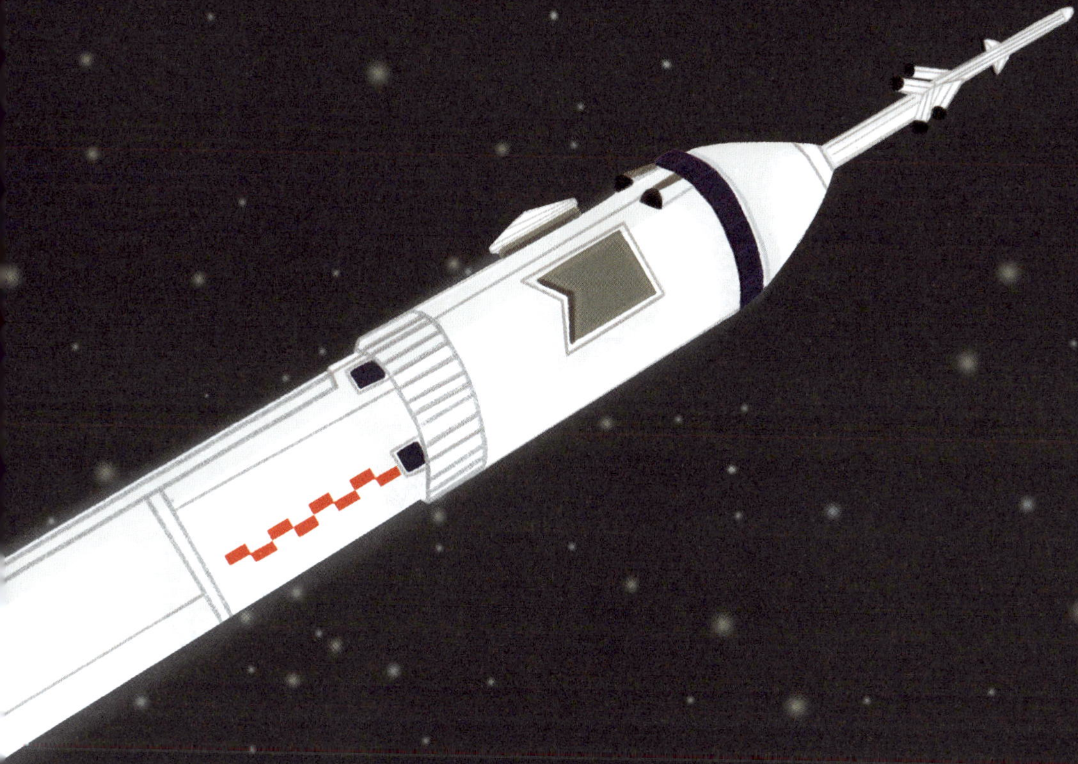

Most scientists believe that the **Kármán line** is where Earth's atmosphere ends and outer space begins. Once a rocket leaves Earth's atmosphere, it must continue to use its power to overcome Earth's gravity. The rocket also needs to be moving at **extremely fast speeds!**

Once in outer space, the manned spacecraft is released from the rocket. Astrodynamics engineers have designed reusable spacecraft to take people into space. They currently transport **cargo** and astronauts to and from the space station.

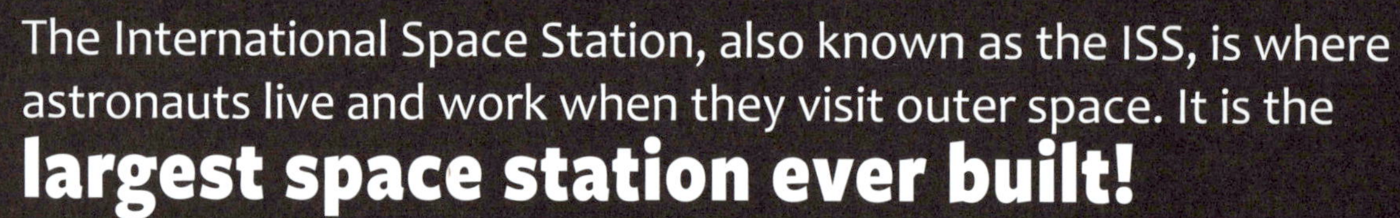

The International Space Station, also known as the ISS, is where astronauts live and work when they visit outer space. It is the **largest space station ever built!**

It was taken up to space piece-by-piece. **Spacewalking** astronauts were sent to put it together, while floating in **orbit**! Astrodynamics engineers helped to design and build this spacecraft, and make sure it stays in the right orbit.

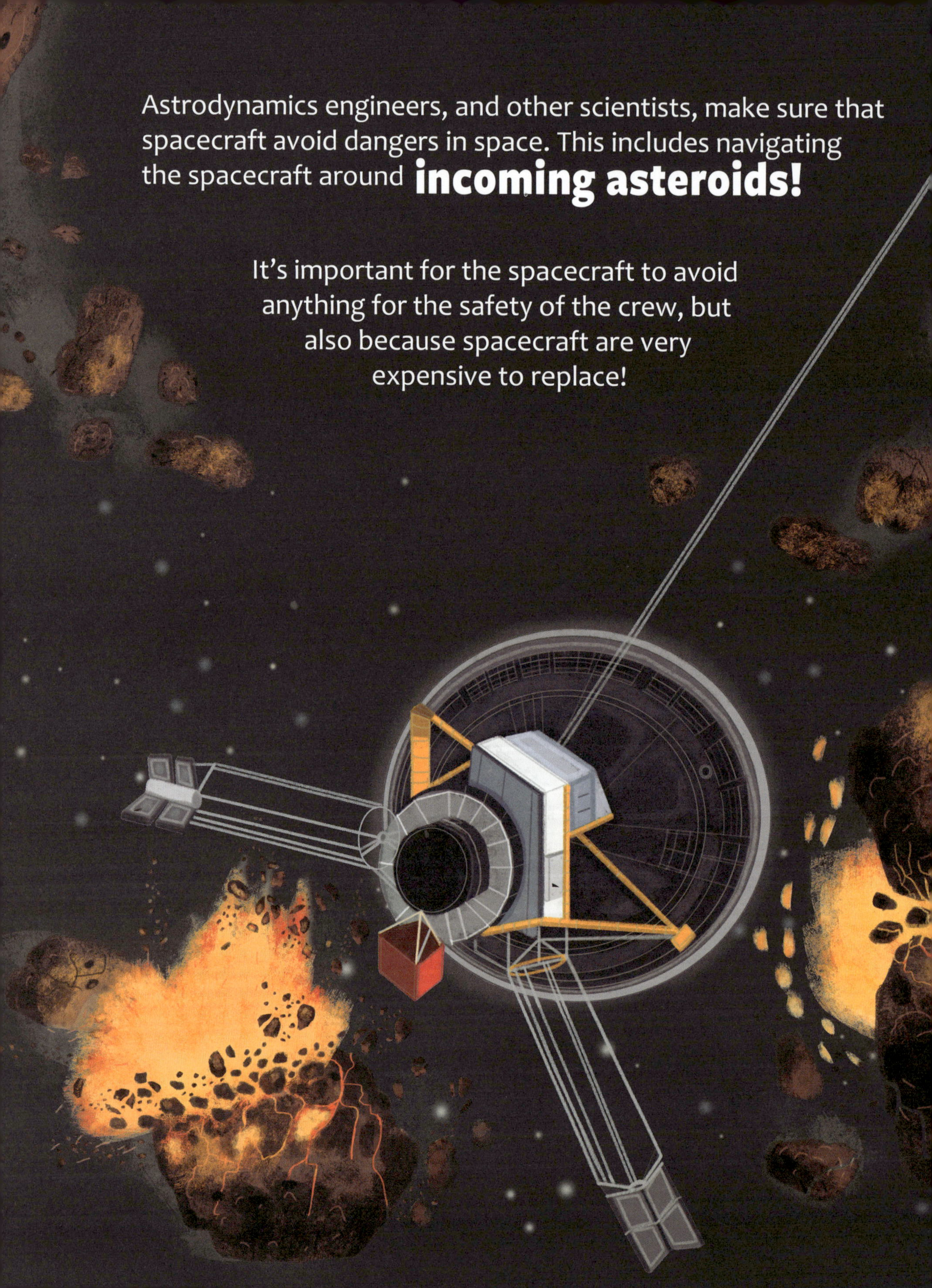

Astrodynamics engineers, and other scientists, make sure that spacecraft avoid dangers in space. This includes navigating the spacecraft around **incoming asteroids!**

It's important for the spacecraft to avoid anything for the safety of the crew, but also because spacecraft are very expensive to replace!

Spacecraft are able to help us learn so much more about our **solar system**. As satellites orbit the Sun, they collect lots of information about planets, moons, and any objects they find there.

They are able to take clear images of planets, and help scientists understand their size, what they are made of, and just how far away they are. But modern spacecraft don't just explore our solar system...

They also explore **interstellar space!**

Interstellar space is the big, mysterious area found outside our solar system. Scientists want to discover as much as they can about what lies here!

Voyager 1 was the first spacecraft to enter interstellar space after crossing through the **heliopause**.

Astrodynamics engineers don't just work with human-made satellites, they study **natural satellites** too! Our Moon is a natural satellite that orbits Earth. Planets, asteroids, and comets are also considered natural satellites.

The Cassini spacecraft discovered that Saturn has the most natural satellites of any planet in our solar system.

It has over 200 moons!

In mission control, spacecraft are closely tracked by scientists. They can sometimes fix them using computers when they go wrong, from here on Earth! Astrodynamics engineers spend lots of time guiding spacecraft to ensure a successful mission. They are the **unsung heroes of science!**

The future of human space travel is filled with exciting possibilities. Astrodynamics engineers are working toward designing spacecraft that can take humans further into space. They even have plans to walk on Mars one day...

The journey will take many months, but is an exciting next step for space exploration. Astrodynamics engineers aren't just launching spacecraft; they are helping us learn more about our solar system, and beyond!

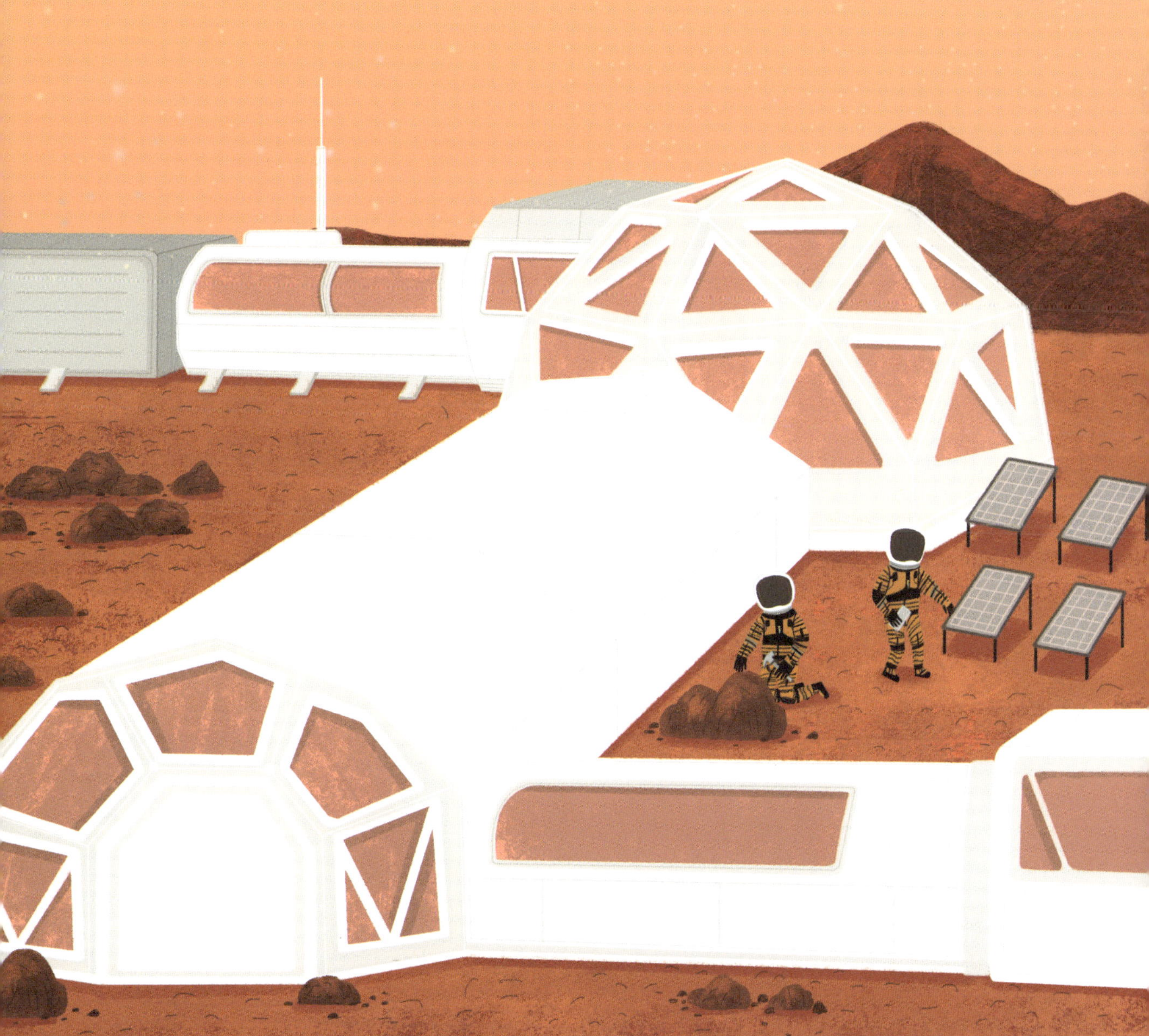

Incredible SPACECRAFT

Now we know all about what astrodynamics engineers do, what type of spacecraft have they helped to send and bring back from space? Here's just a few of the most impressive ones!

The longest single flight was... SKYLAB 4

Skylab 4 was a space station that hosted astronauts for 84 days in 1973, making it the longest single space mission at that time. The crew conducted science experiments and enjoyed the view of Earth!

The first Chinese manned spacecraft was... SHENZHOU 5

Launched in 2003, Shenzhou 5 carried the first Chinese astronaut, Yang Liwei. The spacecraft was on its mission for 21 hours in total, allowing it to orbit Earth 14 times.

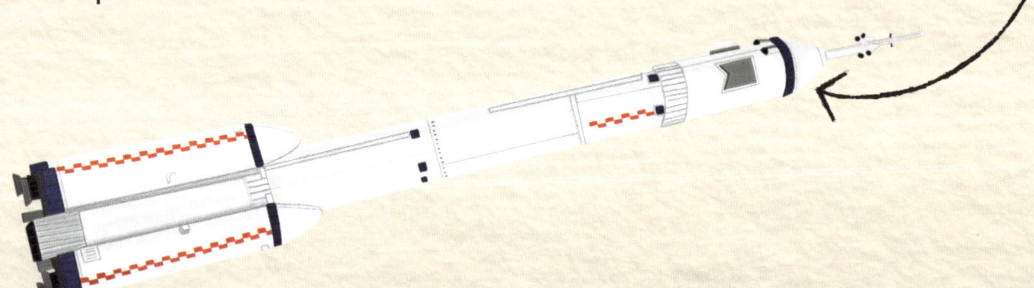

The first human mission on the Moon was... **APOLLO 11**

Apollo 11 Lunar Module was the first spacecraft to take astronauts to the surface of the Moon. It landed on July 20, 1969. Neil Armstrong and Buzz Aldrin were the first humans to walk on the surface of the moon!

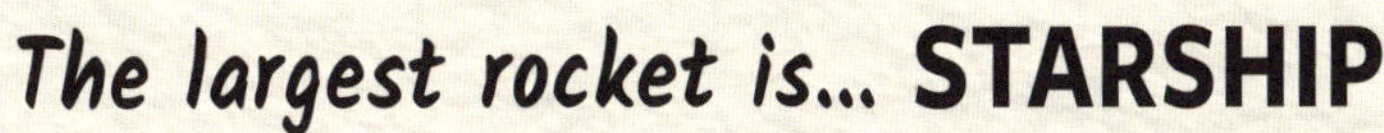

The largest rocket is... **STARSHIP**

Starship is the largest reusable rocket built so far! It's designed to transport people to Mars, and other destinations in space, making it perfect for adventures beyond Earth.

The farthest spacecraft is... **VOYAGER 1**

Launched in 1977, Voyager 1 remains the farthest a spacecraft has gone in outer space. This impressive spacecraft has discovered many incredible things on its long journey.

Amazing

ASTRODYNAMICS FACTS

Astrodynamics allows many impressive things to happen in space, but what else is there to know about this exciting, futuristic science?

THE FASTEST HUMAN-MADE OBJECT IN SPACE HAS BROKEN ITS OWN RECORD!

The fastest human-made object ever is the Parker Solar Probe. It travels at an incredible 394,736 miles per hour (635,266 km per hour)!

IT WOULD TAKE NINE YEARS TO WALK TO THE MOON!

It usually takes about three days for a crewed spacecraft to reach the Moon, but if you were able to walk to it, it would take around 3,200 days!

SATELLITES CAN HELP US UNDERSTAND CLIMATE CHANGE!

Satellites in space can help us understand **climate change** on Earth. They do this by tracking changes to ice around the world.

THE INTERNATIONAL SPACE STATION COMPLETES AN ORBIT OF EARTH EVERY 90 MINUTES!

During that time, part of the Earth can be seen in complete darkness and the other part in bright daylight.

VOYAGER 1 IS THE FARTHEST HUMAN-MADE OBJECT FROM EARTH!

It is currently over 15 billion miles (24 million km) away! It's exploring interstellar space, and sending back important new information about what can be found there.

GLOSSARY

Artificial – made by humans.

Asteroids – small, rocky objects that orbit the Sun, mostly found in the asteroid belt between Mars and Jupiter.

Atmosphere – the gases that surround a planet.

Cargo – items carried in vehicles, such as spacecraft.

Climate change – a change in the weather conditions over a long time.

Crewed – a spacecraft or mission that has humans on board.

Fuel – materials that are burned to produce energy.

Gravity – the force that pulls objects toward each other, keeping planets in orbit around the Sun and us on the ground.

Heliopause – the surface of the area that surrounds our own solar system; the beginning of deep space. *Need help saying this? Look below!*

Human-made – similar to artificial (see left), made by humans.

Interstellar space – outer space just past the edge of our solar system. *Need help saying this? Look below!*

Kármán line – located about 62 miles (100 km) above sea level, the Kármán line is often considered the edge of space.

Natural satellites – a satellite (see below), that is not human-made, that orbits a planet. The Moon is a natural satellite.

Orbit – the repeated path taken by one object circling around another object in space.

Propellant – a substance used to produce thrust in rockets and engines, helping them to move through outer space.

Satellite – any object that orbits a planet. Satellites can be natural, like moons, or artificial (see left), like the ones we use for communication.

Solar system – the Sun and everything that moves around it.

Spacewalking – when an astronaut moves in space outside of a spacecraft.

HOW DO I SAY?

Astrodynamics
AST-roh-dye-NAM-iks

Astrodynamics Engineers
AST-roh-dye-NAM-iks En-jih-NEERZ

Heliopause
HEE-lee-oh-pawz

Interstellar
in-ter-STEL-er

THE BIG QUESTIONS ANSWERED

**This is more than just a series of books; it is a complete resource.
Accompanying each book is a variety of FREE material to engage curious kids with science.**

www.thebigquestionsanswered.com

Use the QR code to visit the website, download free resources, and discover other books in the series.

On the website, find out incredible things about astrodynamics engineers, including what they do, some of their greatest discoveries, and the people who have made a difference in this field of science.

The material is also available for home or classroom use, supporting all the information in this book.

Teachers' & Parents' Resources
With discussion prompts and questions, extra information, and facts around key topics.

Young Astrodynamics Engineers' Activity Pack
Fun activities for wannabe astrodynamics experts, including creative writing, drawing, word searches, and much, much more.

BEETLE BOOKS

**The Big Questions Answered is published by Beetle Books.
Beetle Books is an imprint of Hungry Tomato Ltd.**

First published in 2025 by Hungry Tomato Ltd
F15, Old Bakery Studios, Blewetts Wharf, Malpas Road,
Truro, Cornwall, TR1 1QH, UK.

ISBN 9781835691397

A CIP catalog record for this book is available from the British Library.

With thanks to:
Editors: Millie Burdett and Holly Thornton
Senior Designer: Amy Harvey
The team at Beehive Illustration

Information in this book is up to date as of the time of writing.

Printed and bound in China.

Picture Credits:
(t = top, b = bottom, m = middle, l = left, r = right)
Wikipedia: By NASA - https://images.nasa.gov/details-sl4-143-4706; originally from http://grin.hq.nasa.gov/ABSTRACTS/GPN-2000-001055.html, Public Domain, https://commons.wikimedia.org/w/index.php?curid=6449599 32mr; By DimaLopatin1999 - Own work, CC BY-SA 4.0, https://commons.wikimedia.org/w/index.php?curid=114413632 33br.
Shutterstock: Artsiom P 35mr; Claudio Caridi 35bl; Mechanik 35tl; Shutterstock AI 34bl; Vadim Sadovski 34tr.